# *Look Again*

## Shaykh Fadhlalla Haeri

Zahra Publications

Published by Zahra Publications
ISBN (Printed Version): 978-1-919826-98-1

Designed and typeset in South Africa by Mizpah Marketing Concepts
Cover design by Mizpah Marketing Concepts
Cover Image supplied by: Margi Lake

http://www.sfhfoundation.com
www.zahrapublications.com
© Zahra Publications

# About the Author

Born in Karbala, Iraq, Shaykh Fadhlalla Haeri, comes from several generations of religious and spiritual leaders. After several years living and working in the west, he rediscovered the universal relevance of the Qur'an and Islamic teachings for our present day. His emphasis has been on transformative worship and refinement of conduct, as preludes to the realisation of the prevalence of Divine Grace. He considers that the purpose of life is to know and resonate with the eternal essence of the one and only Lifegiver—Allah

# Acknowledgements

Thank you to Muna Bilgrami, Abbas Bilgrami, Leyya Kalla, Muneera Haeri, Zaheer Cassim, Dr Zaheer Adham, Margi Lake and a special thanks to Hashim Ismail.

# Contents

# It Is For You

No neglect or oversight

no one spared

perfect destiny

beyond judgement

beyond perfection

what else could happen

other than the happening

chains of events

known and unknown

produce the outcome

intended or otherwise

witnessed by consciousness

before personification

debasement or glorification

So please read it

for what it is

clear and honest

That is reading at its best

# The Cherry Tree

Glorious morning

dancing clouds

adding colours

to earth, sky and

the cherry tree

offering its gifts

to birds, humans, ants

and others

to celebrate life

for life's sake

# Obsession

The big question

origin of existence

source of dependence

obsessed

with origin and

illusion of separation

and cause of connectedness

root of all obsession;

for eternal life

the perpetual origin

# Allah

Allah

Light of lights

Light of the heart

cosmic lights and their shadows

here, there and everywhere

beaming at

countless universes

fused by Oneness

in absence and

presence

Allah

# What Is It?

Expressed

by light, colour and form

movement and vibration

presenting itself

through constant change

and transformation

revealed as new existence

visible and hidden

emanating

from essence –

that which Is

perpetual

That is what it is

# Missing

I shall miss you

confused by fears

bleakness of absence

always missing

always desiring

something

always in need of

something

The original light

from the Source

revealing all

whilst shadows

conceal and veil

make us yearn

for what is imagined

as missing

# Rosa Damascena

Heavenly scent

from a flimsy flower

a metaphor of

appearances hiding

secrets and whispers

nature's trials and deceptions

defying habits of mind

drifting thoughts

and expectations

poison can heal

and your friend is a foe

and thorns hide the

secret of a rose

# Doings

There is much to do

undo and redo

tasks and mistakes

patterns of cosmic beingness

where actor and action

were at one with

boundless nothingness

before the illusion

of desires and strivings to

know and go beyond

success and failure

and other comedies

produced by minds

energised by

light of heart

# Inclusively Exclusive

To focus

to separate

to exclude

to include

absorbed

to connect or disconnect

with something or another

then lose all

unto exclusiveness

then to inclusiveness

aspects of allness

motherness and fatherness

colours of

Oneness

# Where To?

I now know

illusion is my home

and distraction my profession


Now I am nowhere

under the illusion

of getting somewhere

driven by hope to benefit

and lose in time

a future that embraces

separation and distance

obliterating absence

and other ailments

past or future

then

more stars appear

from mother Oneness

showing paths of

dispersion and separation

declaring another possibility

of existence

and presence

of

perpetual Oneness

# Four Substances

Fragile life

yet tenacious

pulsating between

dualities within unity

modified by chemistry, physics and biology

rearranged by

air

earth

water and

fire

alchemy for life

temporary and permanent

four seasons

woven within

the same space and time

# Perfect Outcome

Choice

merges with

determined

outcome


Illusion of freedom

nourishes intention

and action

with consequences

expected or not

fate or divine will

Perfect outcomes always

if only you can read

the writings of the

perfect author

# With The Beloved

Now

go faster

much faster

beyond speed and motion

before now

or existence

or presence

or absence

Soon you will go past

all illusions, inclusions and exclusions

There is the

abode of the beloved

cosmic home of love

where all are one with

the one Beloved

# Worshipping

Chanting filled the air

we worship you

the real one

the True One

not creation

or other illusions

the real you

the author

of the cosmic dance

and other music

There is only

You

# Politics

Who had done it?

By what authority?

Justice and generosity

masked absurdity

labelled as democracy

theocracy

or other deceptions

masquerading realities

pretending and bluffing

weak minds

dim hearts

and the world's

sleepwalkers

# Remembrance

To recall

far and near

inner and outer

temporary and permanent

traces in space

lights and sounds

from sacred silence

descending in

grace and delight

now

aware of its

Presence

Now

# Breath

All continues

pulsating in time

creating its presence

close or far

shadows dressed up

as substance from here

from nowhere

encompassing all breaths

breathlessly

celebrating

each one

touched by life

in and out

within the embrace

of grace of

Divine breath

# Dependencies

Everybody loves it

striving for

power and autonomy

will to control

connected through love

connecting with ease

or difficulty

But at all times

the dependent self

shadow of the soul

needy and deceptive

passing realities

a universe of co-dependencies

vanishing as clouds

with faint traces

upon the vast sky

self-dependent

# True Language

Often silently

sometimes aloud

mouth and body

spoke

sometimes from heart

Self and soul speak

the original language

connector of all

before alphabet

and boundaries

prescribed by language

and noisy sounds

where silence

declared all

# Insight

To hear, see and perceive

understand and explore more

other senses reinforce

evolving identity

in new lands

skies, caves and valleys

sights and

insight and lights

pointing to the real

where the sun

hides all the stars

and truth

prevails  over all

# Divine Obsession

Connect, continue and be conscious

at one

with the

original force

returning everything to itself

divine obsession

Oneness

# Expressions Of Love

Love of life

good life

love of now

and all of now's future

present in the moment

flowing by love

along the sacred thread

returning past, present and future

to the sacred now


Life is within eternity

within constant continuity

before and within all

all in all

expressing a colour

of love

# Ho' Opono' Pono

The self

reveals itself

repenting

'I am sorry'

then connecting

'forgive me'

then uplifting

'I love you'

Then

gratitude

to existence

and

'thank you'

and thanks

to all

# Connection

Together

to be gathered

as in origin

before anything

as is now

as is ever

known or unknown

together or separate

ever connected

in origin

now

and forever

# Don't Miss It

To miss an opening

for real life

stillborn

dead but living

Don't miss it

Don't talk or reflect

Don't think or meditate

Just don't miss it


Perpetual life

boundless

with or without you

acknowledging

original life–

Don't miss it

# The Real Doer

The will to live

traced in actions

desires and needs

impressions in existence

calling for conclusions

uniting beginnings

and ends

then repeating patterns

dancing dualities

shades of light

illumined by

the Real Doer

# Pleasure Of Pain

Tearful eyes

looking at

newborn son

placed upon breast

emerged from

pain and pleasure

a new emergence

to face life's puzzles

to face unknowns

seeking to know

Who is who?

What is what?

From the mother's womb

to the veil of body and mind

a journey to

the Illumined Heart

Sides Of The Coin

One side reads:

Be still

joyfully

die in peace


One side reads:

Go for it

urgently

rush and push


The coin's real value

is beyond

any measure

a sacred treasure

fortunate are those

who ever know that

# To Connect

She listened to stones

talked to weeds

absorbed the breeze

talked to heavens

smiled at earth

A good place, maybe

for guests like us

heavenly dust

earthbound for a while

ever-connected

to origin

and destiny

# Tricks Of Life

Some are simple

others complex

a few miracles

a deceptive universe

But habits continue

tricks become magic

life drifts on

elusive and real

all temporary

pointing to the

permanent

What a trick!

# Rise And Fall

The leaves

are falling

end of a cycle

a new landing

silently announcing

new beginning

already progressing

towards a new rise

and what rises falls

completing  patterns

within perfect

stillness

moving

up and down

breath of the living

# Entrapments

Trapped again

on a rocky shore

sea rising

closing escapes

Where now?

And how?


Trapped by sight

sound and mind

by love and hate

by fear and sorrow

and countless other illusions

knowledge or ignorance

pleasure or pain

and by even the idea of

a divine trapper

# Please Stay Forever

I need you

now and later

I fear loneliness

your absence

my sorrow


Please promise

to stay

forever

and longer

without end

for I only love

the Permanent

# Exploration

The unknown

without landmarks

without boundaries–

Is that our origin?

Is that God's domain?

The sage said

there is only God


He also said  discovery begins

when separation ends

and Reality is realised

containing all


I want to know that

But the sage has gone

Who can help me now?

# Way Of Rainbow

Desires attained

what next?

To position rainbows

differently

or wear

as a wedding dress

or a shroud

and then melt back

into light

as a rainbow does

# Where Is She Now?

Mother's gone

cried the tearful daughter

no longer present

I can't bear it

I can't cope

She wept some more

absorbed in bleakness

fear and sorrow

loss of hope and now despair

why to live?

As for reasons of death

the question is ignored

for now at least

for mother has just died

and no one knows why

# Generosity To All

Primal sounds

sights and insights

carried by lights

to destiny

the sacred breath

giving existence to

everything possible

and more

past, present and future

and beyond

the ultimate generosity

to one

and all

# All Or Nothing

The limitless

beyond measure

timelessness

endless now

and before all

and after all

where all

and nothing

in cosmic embrace

and all else

is nothing

except that which

has it all

# Trusting

Beyond reason

primal acceptance

connecting

unifying

this is where ease

flows

perpetually

This most desirable state

is the real you

within you

if you embrace it with

unconditional love

then and only then

can I trust

You

# Favouritism

Downward and upward

changing succession

one place and one time

better than others

one person or another

one meal or another

one finger or another

one investment or another

one book, one day, one year

one life, one country,

one shirt, one companion,

one situation, one authority


The desired favourite

ever there

if only you are there

# A Temporary Secret

Love of power

knowledge and secrets

keep it or share it

Like all values

it grows or fades

whilst uncertainty remains

all desires too

grow and fade

But why?

To test the patience

of dying patients

knowledge with ignorance

love of life with

inevitability of death

where all secrets vanish

# Both Of Me

Pursuing pleasure and goodness

relentlessly

within measures and

beyond measure

new and old

ever-changing

as does the mirror –

but which is me?

How can I be scattered?

Even the shadow is

loyal and devoted

to its light

but one day

I too

may be at one

with the soul

within me

# Birthday

No one asks Why?

What are you celebrating?

What is the cause to rejoice!?

Is it only old age?

Years of suffering, confusion and consumption!

So absurd that no one asks …

Well done!

You are one more year

But then what?

You stop counting

as your soul has moved

back home

in a new birth

without the burden

of body and mind

a liberated soul

# Troubles

You trouble me

I announced

to myself

Yes, you

disturb me

burden me

hurt me

distract me

from the Real me

re-inventing new stories,

new desires and new guilts

re-inventing distraction

from being at one

with me

# An Image

Pampered

head to toe

to appear beautiful

gentle and smooth


As for the light of the heart

postponed by self obsession

How do I look

at least for now?

Forget the rest

I have no time now

I love my new hair

at least for now

a new fashion

now

my new image

for now

# Flow Of Life

Hang on

Hold on

Focus and connect

or else

lose all

your self

your duty

honour and loyalty

and more

shame and blame

birth and death

and new tricks

but for now

just hang on life

ever-flowing

ever there

# Magnanimity Of Spirit

Here is my list of priorities

Clothes are important

food

home

friends

my intentions and actions

and the way I walk

even the way I sleep

even my silence

I can even say more


So where can you hide?

How and from whom?

But your practice has been

to hide from your real self

that which know all

does not sleep or die

Yet you still try

to hide, deceive and deny

All of this is also due to

generosity of spirit

which says with a smile

there is no escape.

# Cosmic Trap

Trapped again

in a new pattern

woven by space and place


Water, sand and stones

trapping the tide

pretending to move

following the moon

to perceive the end

Truth itself

beyond measure or wisdom

Light of Reality

illumined by a magnificent Grace

Source of all traps

# Repetition

Just repeat

whatever

a song

a sigh

a wink

repeat for life

whatever

constant

forever

like life itself

continuous

but ever fresh

# True Life

That man

saved me

killed me


When I looked again

gone like me

the work done


This is the real story

Life with no illusions

quest with no conclusion

Life celebrating itself

with no concern for

time or place

or who is there

or not there

# A Repeated Tale

Humans

singular and plural

same and different

mingled biographies

each with a story

same but different


But for now

I release my story

so I  can die

in peace

complete and content

smiling at my inner self

Is that possible?

Without fear

regrets or grief?

# Polite People

Much effort

to conceal ignorance or discordance

denials or fears

fueled by self pity

self-concern and self regret

more and more of self!

enhanced by identity

reinforced by polite people

energized by their noise

revitalized with ceremonies

communal sharing and caring

Meanwhile the love dove

sings its heart out

with no concern

for appearances

or politeness

# Friendly Mirror

Who was she?

A sister or a mother

or was it a father

or both or neither!

Only partly true!

What experiences life

will also go

through death

only you belong to neither

All that appears or hides

rejection and acceptance

are shades of

the perfect original light

# Accidental Country

He formed a circle

with both hands

Poor country

with a rich heart

and a complex flag

appearing important

but no one really cares


Poor people

but proud

Poor history

with cruel rulers

like God

feared and loved

complex

like the flag

The new heroes rise

from zero

and then back again

while confused people are trapped in darkness


Political slogans

economic absurdities

confusing lies

failing on most issues

except football

and environmental degradation

and don't forget

obesity with malnutrition

The poor country

with a big heart

# Jerusalem

The golden city

for perfect life

for God's children

the city above the hill

In the promised land


That was an idea

whose reality is

a seductive toxic trap

for the blind at heart

dreaming love

but living in fear and sorrow

dreaming victory

for the chosen people

by a mythical exclusive God

whilst the city weeps blood

# Relocate

Desiring change

a new life

less baggage

less errors

less trials

But how? And where?

A change of scenery

change of mind

and heart

away from locality

a taste of universality

a spark of infinity

A relocation

To where?

Somewhere that is

not a place

# Help

Will it be alright?

The tearful eyes

questing

reassurance

Will I be happy?

Will you still

love me

after we die?

I want to be sure

Please help me

to remain

happy for ever

Oh God

Please help

# Begging For Change

After disasters

pleading at the door

weeping for mercy


Today

Now

for better destiny

with dignity

with honour

for God's sake

for His grace

a change

from the past

for better future

please God

bring the change

# True Self

Be yourself

They all say that

Ignorant folks sounding credible

You try and fail

more confused

Where, What and Who is this self?


Absurd wisdom

tiresome

whilst suffering constantly

stumbling within shadows

weaping for the soulmate

perhaps that is what they refer to

as the real self

My soul

# Sound Waste

It is too noisy here!

Wasted energy

pretending to communicate!

expressing frustration

labelled as self expression

damaging silence

and sacred stillness

and the immensity of the instant

avoided by noise or action

or other distraction

For who can take the power of

sacred presence?

We are experts in

postponement and absence

# More Stories

Only one story to tell

in many versions

sparks of the real

the rest is bad fiction


There was one

There was no one

Other than the One

there is no one


What you perceive

colours of the One

appear as sight

pointing to insights

towards the One

the only One

The mind provides

reason

and other illusions

named as reason

accepting and rejecting

good and bad

Monkeys swing on trees

Humans? More like

sleepwalkers

Humans swing

confused between head and heart

complain and blame

mixing shadows and light

claiming sincerity

to know and awaken

whilst darkness is their home

and noisy stories

poison the air

# The Way Out

Where is the end?

Who can stop it?

I only care for now

I have been before in this struggle

I have become an expert

of return to bleakness

I have followed

different paths and teachers

with promises that recede further

or embrace self delusion

and

religious coziness

elitist smugness

So please for now

just take me out of me

I have suffered enough

# Waking Up

Stop all and be silent

Then be still completely


Be at one with Nothingness

beyond and before

existence and creation

and that is where your

origin and light resides

and then only now you know

the ignorance of sleep walkers

where you emerged from

# Touch Of Truth

Devastated by truth

all covers blown off

imposters, deceivers

and other pretenders

all stopped

Stillness and peace prevailed

for an instant

everyone knew

the perfect end here and now

as in the beginning

then comes the next moment

with its new

fears and sorrows

# More Tricks

Some were simple and new

others inherited

Cultural or habitual

a few tricks we like

such as gifts and kindness

others we denounce

all are creational delusions

enhanced by self deception

and dark minds and hearts

crying for awakening

and the perfect

conclusion

# Presents From Presence

Gift of delights

from sacred silence and its

effulgent presence


All in all

All and all

not here or there

just presence


Overflowing generosity

and more

including what is not desired

and more

proving sacredness

of presence

# Play Of Time

In a rush?

Then Stop!

If slow

then hasten slowly

stop and be still

and then let it resume


Your life flows

with ease or difficulty

Life flows

breathing in and out

your reference

the gaps between

stillness is

your touchstone

and silence your abode

# Honest Testing

Devastated by truth

all covers removed

your reason

and other pretenses

devastated by truth

all dualities removed

by the light of singularity


Now you know

the end of no end

clear and everlasting

when everything else

stopped

# What Time?

There is no time left

There was no time anytime

no part-time or full-time

no present time

no past time

no time

Now you may feel confused

only that is in time?

your own invention

your own illusion of time

But when grace gifts you the elixir of timelessness

then you stop all questions concerning

all that is made in time.

# Gravity

The pull

towards its heart

its core

personal expression

of Unity

Singularity

Cosmic Reality

in its full embrace

of all that is profound

includes the presence

or absence of gravity

# The Cry

I shall cry

I shall weep, oh I shall weep.

With or without

reason

I know

I shall cry

My throat tells me

the moist eyes

flooding its reason

without a Noah's ark

I shall only cry

I can only cry

and then float

in the new river

# Sparks Of Truth

Silently

in tears

cleansing

today's deception.

Why me again?

In pain again

between darkness and light

between birth and death

between shades of lies

strung along

changing consciousness

revealing its

Truth

sometime silently

sometimes aloud

# Original Abode

The separate particle

is somebody now

suffering from confusion

longing for

contentment and peace

where and when?


'Na Koja Aabaad'

the perfect state

not in a place

or time

the perfect abode

here, now and ever

but nowhere

as you think

# Fate

Not clear at first

accept or reject

give in

accommodate

or negate

to turn or not to move

losing your will

or asserting it

confused at

the gate of perfect fate

within time and space

and before all

# Back Home

Expectations

of  a better life

without fear, sorrow

or disappointments

a loving home

a welcome guest

without questions or expectations

the cosmic home

and its earthly metaphor

# Quest

I feel safe with you

the heart spoke

Take me somewhere

not the old place

somewhere new

where age is unknown

and time not arrived

and mind not imagined

and the real me

like pure life

with no needs or desires

the original quest

flowing along its perfect destiny

# Cosmic Fireworks

When a star shines

the universe celebrates

the star radiates

its journey a cosmic reminder

mystery of governance

and changing perfection

where the unseen

reveals and conceals

with beginnings and ends

celebrating itself

# Whispers Of Flute

The flute tells its stories

in whispers and silence

telling its story

in sighs and lament

nostalgia and melancholy

asking for directions

to the real home

and reasons for being lost

The flute re-tells

note after note

puzzles of life

beginning to be at one

with light of life

# Full Life

Zoroaster smiled

brighter sun

bigger moon

total presence


Old self drowning

in its lake of tears

pleading to reach

the shore of trust

and presence

grace of perpetual life

brightness

greater than all

suns and moons

# Love's Hold

Forms follow their meaning

Answers love the question

that gave birth to them

Effects love their causes

Ends embrace their beginnings

Separations love togetherness

Darkness points to its light

Connections hold together

by the Light of lights

that permeates and holds all

Lights of love

# To Be

The night wept

sighed and then threatened

to live

longer than time

The day pronounced hope:

the lights of the universe

within you

Let your heart shine, and disclose

song after song

Harmony will complete itself

the story will remain

endless in origin

ever present

perfect beingness

# Concealed Deceptions

Asked about control

I knew the trick

Nothing

And then again – 'What do you want?'

My pretending smile

concealed a million desires, some new, fresh

others ancient lost in time

Then again, how much?

The sky is vast, passions too

fireballs hidden behind rose bushes

truth within falsehood

polite friendly gestures

taught by a hyena

circus trained

by robot monkeys

dressed up as guides and teachers

and other motivational preachers

or business leaders

or political appeasers

self-assured

absorbed in the fog and darkness

of  everyday life

and  other shades of ignorance

confused minds

dark hearts and delusions

announcing

business as usual

We are a great success

# Fire Language

Put out the fire

the trees cried

but a burning bush said:

Fire is life

it gives life

and takes it away

An honest cycle

like a burning passion

yearning for oneness

consumed in the dance

and the endless lament of the lonely gypsy

whilst the fire of love

expresses itself

in the language of its passion

# Light Of The Heart

If our world is not enough

Nor is the universe

Where do ambitions end?

Where is your destiny?

When nothing is enough

What does the heart say?

Lose yourself!

Relieved from all ambitions

only the awakened are

at one with the Light

of the heart

# Confidence

Confidence

alliance

reliance

trust

content

with the moment

certain

all is well

governed

by perfections

# Original Embrace

Connected by knowledge

unified by love

at one

at peace

beginnings and end

meanings and form

inner and outer

chaos and harmony

gathered

embraced by the One

the essence of all

# The Story

Give me

the full story

complete

without space or time

without

beginnings or ends

the full story

direct from its author

self-completing

all-embracing

eternal

the Real story

# Questions

Why, how, where, when?

And more

Such as who am I?

And what is the end?

And why do I miss home?

Where and what is the perfect place for me?

When will quests end?

When will

Questions and Answers

return to the silence

of their mother's womb

connected?

# In The Now

Be present

the teacher said

in mind and heart

he said

presence in now

not that which moves

perpetual now

sense nothing

beyond everything

the now that holds everything

at once

forever absent and present

the ever now

# Passion To Know

The question invites the answer

and shadow proves the light

meanwhile the seeker of truth

is confused and frustrated


Cries for help

and the heart whispers

when consumed by fire

questions and answers will vanish

and perfection reveals its cosmic prevalence


Thank God

for such generosity

# Honesty

Truth

overriding shadows

concealment and other tricks

real intention revealed

business disguised as charity

control as love

taking as giving

and other travesties

including

the idea of

hope

# The Sage

Radiating light

love-scented

flow of ease

from a centre of peace

fully connected

fully present

silence says it all

self and soul are one

with no agenda

except unconditional love

for that which is Real and True


Admirers may envy or desire his state

he is just at one

with the sacred state

# Sleepwalkers

Asleep

together

strength in numbers

close together

culture of hope and despair

renouncing dissidents

unlike us

not to be trusted

spoilers of our own play

we don't like them

we are many

we are real

alive on Facebook

and other shadows

# The Way

When asked direction

he pointed all around

then said

Your destination

pointing everywhere

It is all here

There and here

all of space

every place

If not here and now

there and then

It is a path

where all emanates from

and leads back to it

It is

# Potter's Dance

The sun flung its beam

upon the potter's bridge

then weaved its way

along clay creations

hard and soft

ash, mud and water

light and darkness

Then the sun

took the sky

and earth

and all in-between


The potter danced

smashing his way

all is done

and all returns

one by one

to the only One

# Ever Special

I really think

I am different

not like others


Am I not better?

Special, unique and

outstanding

or is it all self deception

to carry on living

in confusion and fear

with vague promise

and elusive hope

suppressing the inner voice

that declares sacredness of existence

emanating and returning

from Oneness

the Ever Special Sacredness

# All Views At Once

Expectations

disappointments

anger, fear,  sadness

and other traps


Why me? you say

Poor you! they say

Something wrong

Why poor you?

Or me?

Why?

Between

fear and hope

where is liberation?

Before death

or any other time

before

cosmic silence

or deafness

or before

infinite beauty

or perfect clarity

beyond reason

beyond all known

or unknown


Past all

personal views

the land of

no views or news

vistas without

constraints

expressing

the perfect

cosmic view

# Why

Why again?

Moving to where?

By what authority?

Without clarity

Nasty habit


The old you

the new old you

the no you

the yes you

different you

all the masks

veiling the Real you

caught between

traces of past

concerns of now

uncertain future

Is that why?

Why?

# Self Fears

The self fears rejection

confrontation

or sublime ascension

A mighty idea

rightening reality

perfect destiny

feared by identity

separation

differentiation

and all other dualities

completing their journey

beyond self and soul

beyond hope and fear

or whatever considered far or near

The self lives in

fear and sorrow

and the soul simply celebrates

# Soulhood

Not from yourself

not due to effort

or pleading or weeping

but a pure gift of grace


Sacred rain

leaves its trace

as soul or spirit

to bring to life

what seemed dead

a song of praise

countless souls

expressing gratitude

with some joy

and some fear

# Soul Speak

Not as you think

unlike anything else

a spark of

divine light

modified and dimmed

connecting earth

to its heavenly origin

speaking

through

souls and spirits

and other unseen

and unknown

life sources

like the stars

disclose a story

# Bas Means Enough

Satisfied

content

overflowing

at one

with light

and primal will

full mastery

of control

by itself

unto itself

BAS!

Enough!

# Prison Or Sanctuary

Alienation is not beautiful

We prefer connection and harmony

But are you at one with your soul?

Is your soul happy

with your body and mind?

Is your soul

happy with you?

Is your body and mind

in constant reference

with your soul?

To honour and obey

your soul is your duty

and purpose

# Directional Randomness

Where are we going?

Why and how?

Unknown start and

Unknowable end

Sounds bleak!

What about evolution?

Surely it is a clear direction

With occasional dips

If it is only random

Then chaos must be the order

True True True!

# Departure

Mother with young children

not ready to leave

to where

who leaves

what stays

what are illusions

where is God's mercy?

Where is love?

And what is the

conclusion?

# Wilderness

Explore, discover

and more

Where is the Truth?

Where is the Real?

Where is the end?

Where was the beginning?

Where is now?

Why this wilderness

aggression and violence

along with

tolerant co-existence

Travel along time

with hope and pray

to stop time

even for a moment

in time

# Lost Soul

A restless soul

troubled soul

confused soul

while pretending to be normal

functional and polite

not trapped

like other sleepwalkers

pretending to be

awake and

living souls

Poor soul!

# Last Return

When I returned

to what is called here

I was still there

but lost all maps

in a misty dark night

The only light

within my heart

guiding softly

back to the start

the source of all

Grace of Oneness

# Lights Of Life

To acknowledge all

all signs, sight and sound

and tastes

and then step aside

Forget all

including yourself

To die in harmony itself

Is to be at one

celebrating life itself

with light that

illumines life

itself

# Hopes

Hoping for better future

Hoping for good outcome

Hoping for better life

Even hoping for end of hope


Hoping to lose

burdens of the past

and fears of the future

and glimpse the presence


That is a worthy list

to celebrate the possible

end

of all

absence

# Constant Need

I need more time

more space

beyond measure

to end all needs

quests and hopes

Then my life

may begin

without end

or any measure

# Look At Me

Please

look at me

It will help me

to know me

to know destiny

to know the moment

to be in contentment


I'd do anything for that

even die for that

That is a worthy death

to be content

with me and you

and know and don't care

Then there is

nothing more

to care for

or not

# One And Another

If there is one

then there is

another

If there is life

there is also death

perplexing twos

prescribing a path

from the One

and unto the One

# Voice Of Silence

Don't explain

Don't speak

Silence expressed all

sparing sound

and wasted time

Absence that contains presence

still within time and space

veiling the sacred face

self-disclosing

always

with or without

obvious ways

# Take Notice

Please look at what I have

for you

Special

for you

and everyone

extra special

not measurable

or describable

extra special

for you

and everyone else

to admire

and love

and  maybe

content

for a moment

# Bird Song

Colorful vibrations

celebrating life

harmony in space

teasing and pleasing

rainbow of life

chirping robin

free of past

or future

free in life

but caught in Life

as we all were

long long time ago

before life time

# Separation

My needs never end

but for now

I don't need you

anymore

for now at least

I think

Now that I know

my needs never end

I think

or is that wrong?

# The Search

Searching

where is love

where is The One

below or above


outward inward

flying forward

Ruh of Truth

reflecting the One


Pleasures and pain

trying in vain

or is this progress?

# Here In Life

Streams of life

constant and effulgent

appearing and returning

as biographies and images

devoted to loyalty

honesty and sincerity


The nasty sting

a reminder of life

traced to the dead bee

life touching life

all reminders of original

perpetual life

pleasurable or painful reminders

of Lights of life

celebrating

its majesty and beauty

# All In All

This is the question!

Bigger than life itself

unending as life itself

bigger than life and death

or appearance and absence

or illusions of achievements

crying out for conclusions

This question is bigger than

the universe itself

It contains all questions

known and unknown

and all answers

mostly unknown – yet

contains all news and views

before feeble minds interfered

distracting and attracting

before Oneness embraced otherness

where light was before life

before time filled up space

before needs and desires

dreamt up climbing ladders

out of confusions that only lead

to more questions

filling up minds and

polluting hearts

whilst the origin of life

smiles upon existence

and its other offsprings

and Light of truth

Illumines all

always

# You And Me

Be kind to me

Admire and love me

I promise to also be kind

as I feel you are mine

I will be kind as I control you

I love to rule and be strong

I love power and confidence

Don't ask how much

love is limitless

if you ask more

I will pretend to listen

All else is deception

rehearsed collectively

named normal or real

and other stupidities

Invented by you and me

# Bondage To Freedom

Ignoring a duty

Missing a message

of Reality

to respond is to know life

and then experience

the honour of being alive


To acknowledge a duty

an expression of gratitude

to grace and favour

an invitation to beauty

and the sacredness

of being bound

to duty

all celebrating the

ever-free soul

# Madly Sane

The eccentric dervish

tolerated as brief visitor

his speech precious

considered confusing

or rare pearls

or simply ignored

Beyond me they said


The sleep walkers dashed by

not their business

their neat minds declared

Some even labelled him mad


An old lady with tarot cards

reflecting the truth declared

his super-sanity

magnifies

our madness

# At One

No distance

no space

no absence

now

continuously

its end is its beginning

but arrives

after many

nows

different nows

declaring

the same

original

Oneness